STYLES OF ELEGANCE

CATALOGUE: Issue 1

ISBN: 9781098875299

REHOBOTH PUBLICATIONS

APOSTLE MARGUERITE

BREEDY-HAYNES

As believers, everything about our lives should be excellent. The way we live and the way we do things should be about excellence. It is important for us to be pointed out by our excellent way of life. God wants His children to look great.

Today I present to you this catalogue of elegance and I believe that wherever you are and whatever lifestyle you come from, God wants you to be an excellent person.

STYLE

GRACE

CLASS

REFINED

SOPHISTICATED

CULTURED

BEAUTY

CHARMING

POLISHED

SUAVE

FLAIR

DASHING

LUXURIOUS

UNIQUE

HIGH-CLASS

EXCLUSIVE

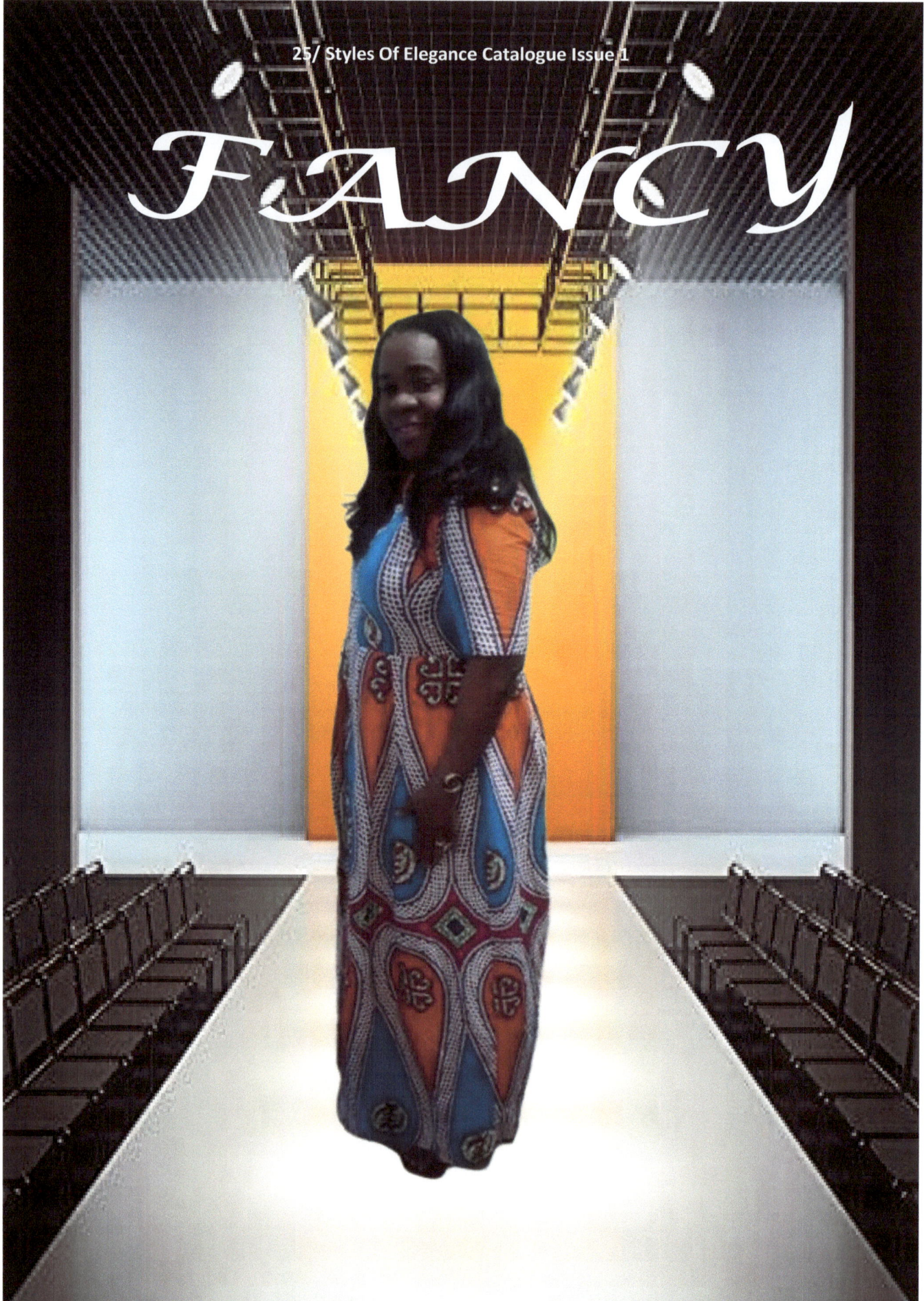

EXPENSIVE

UP-SCALE

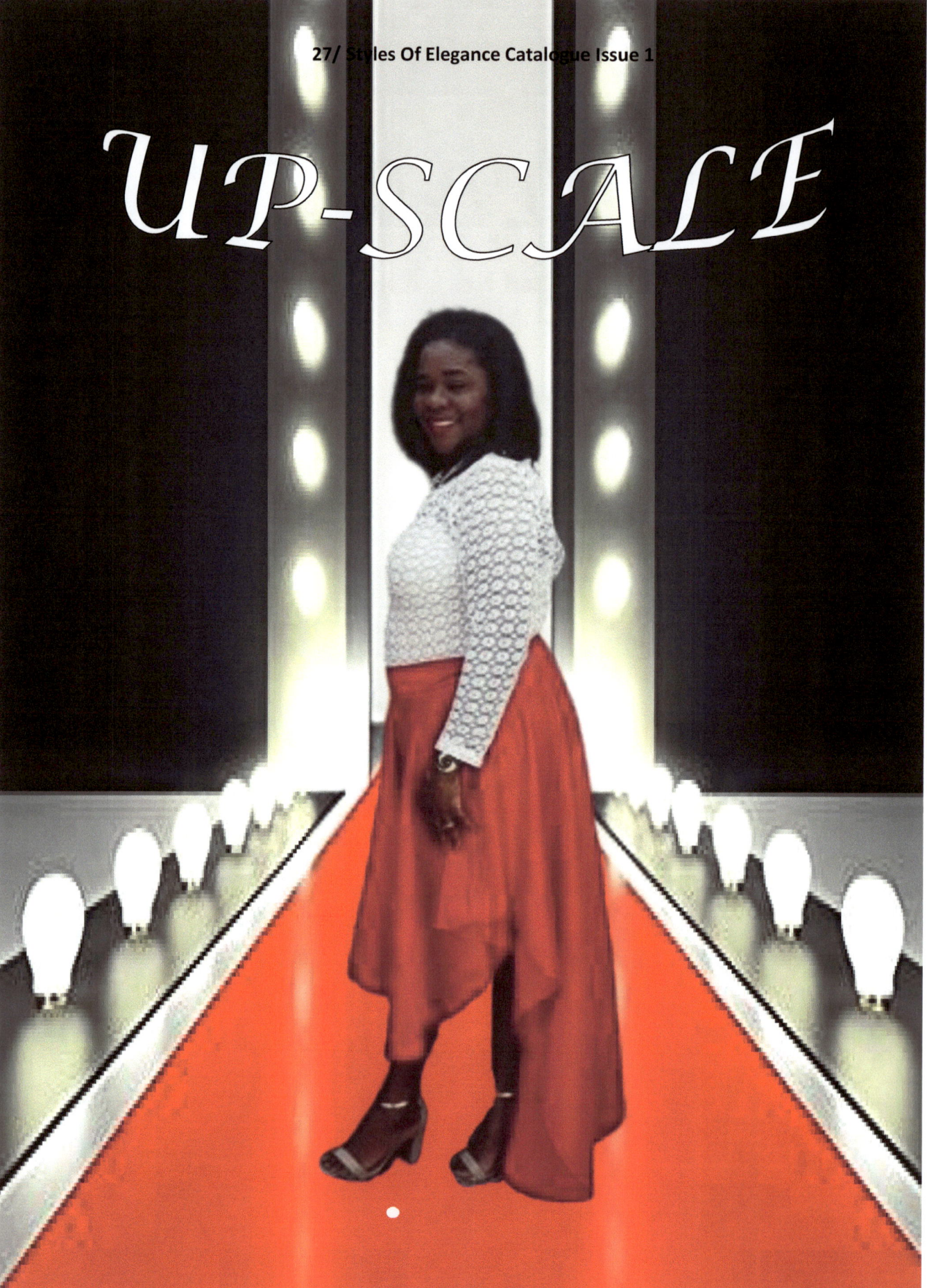

GRACEFUL

SNAZZY

ONE OF A KIND

SWANKY

TREND SETTING

SMOOTH

SWAGGER

HAUTE

© ORG

EDGY

DRESSY

MODERN

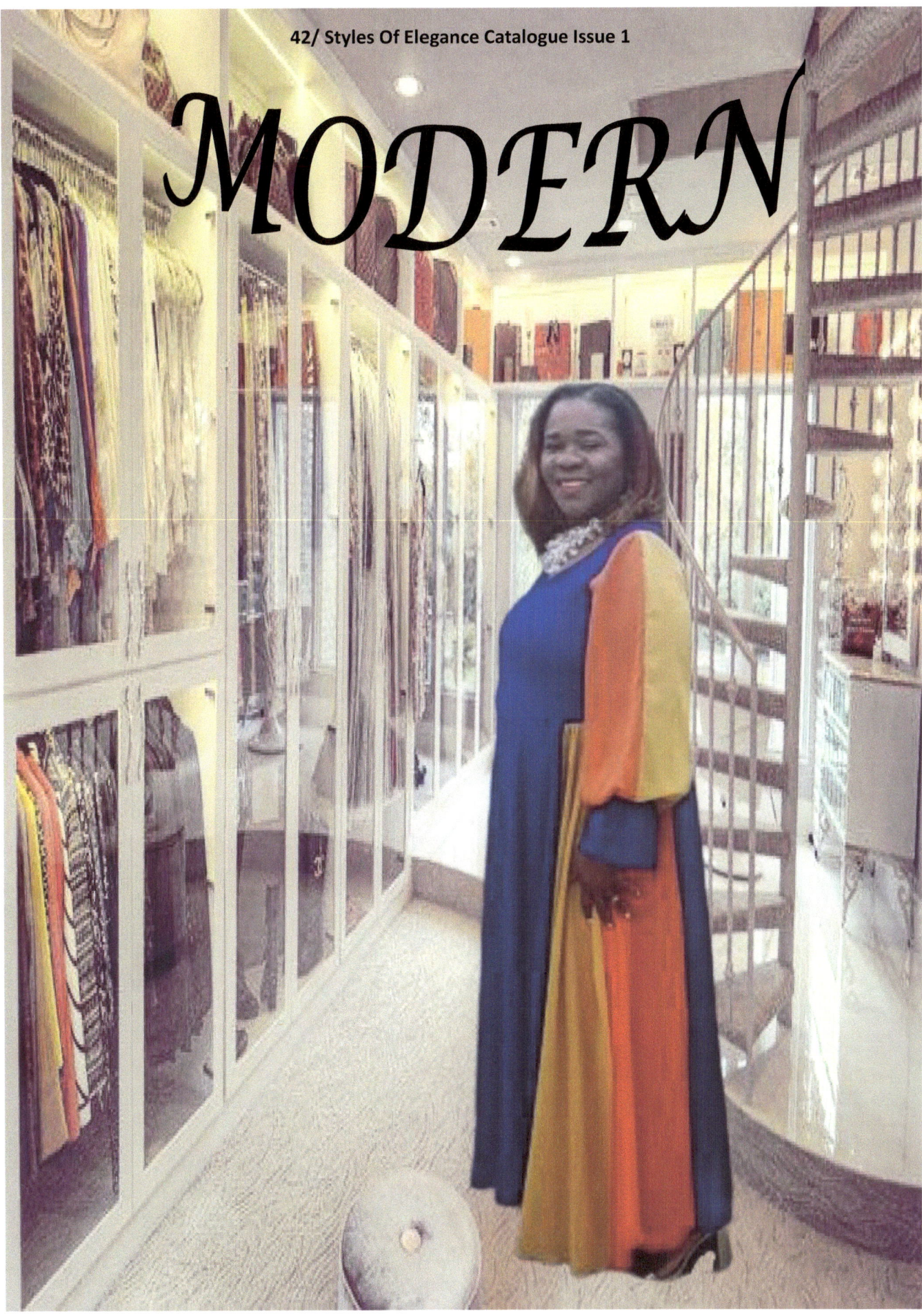

DEBONAIR

FLASHY

DAZZLING

SUPER-COOL

FUTURISTIC

CURRENT

DAZZLER

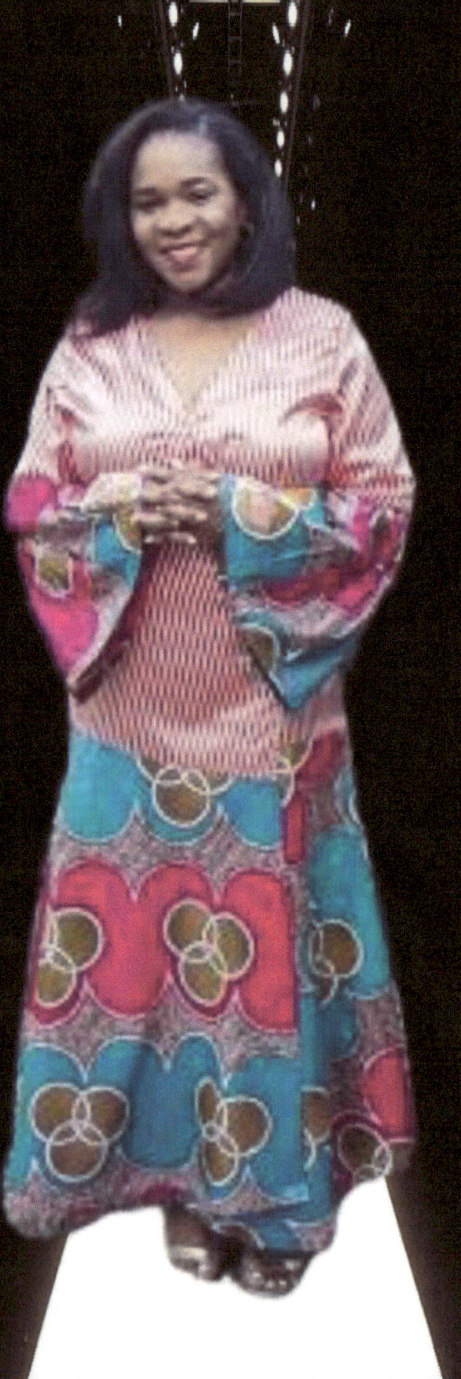

DELIGHTFUL

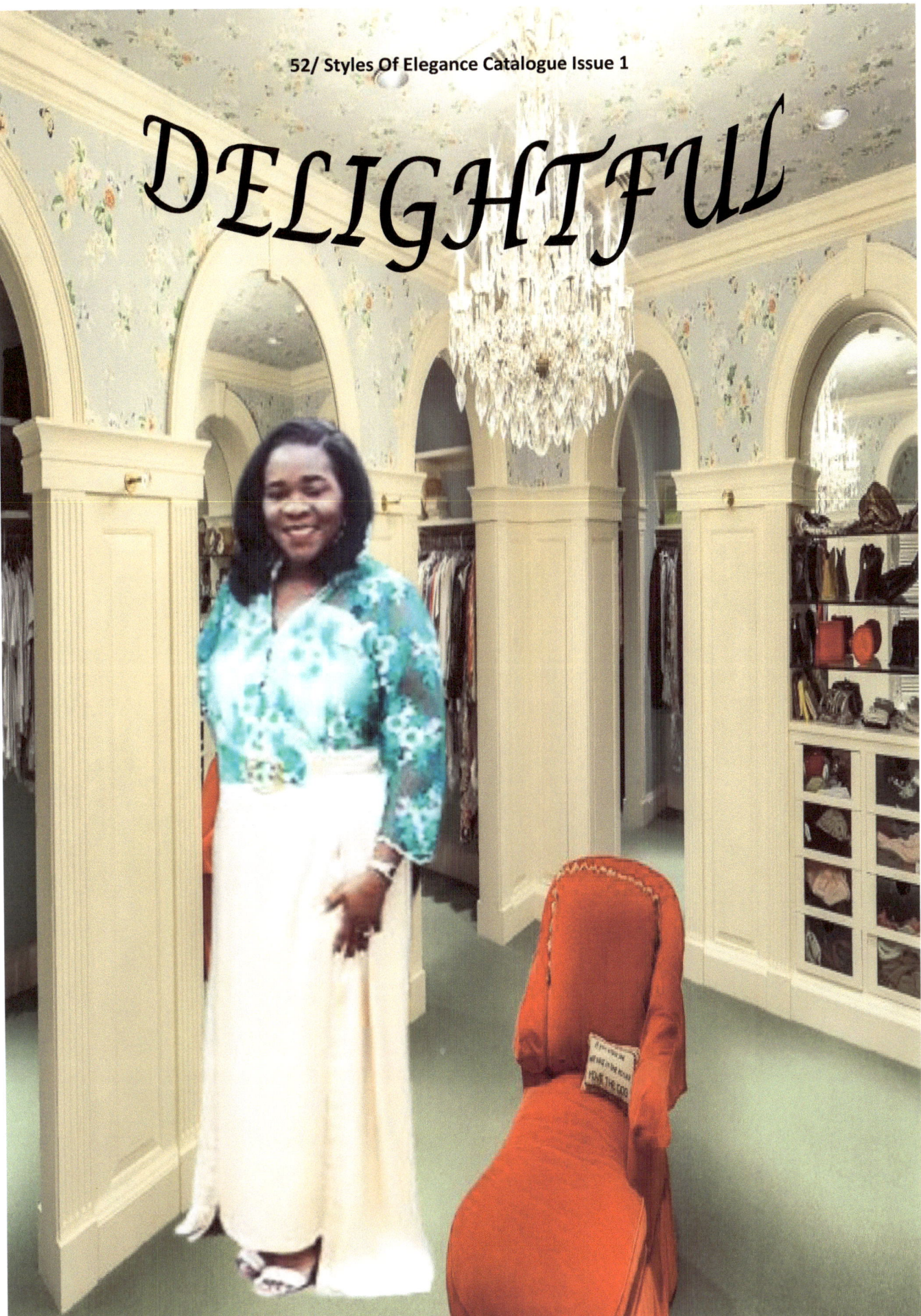

DELIGHTFUL

SIGHTLY

DIVINE

GEORGEOUS

STUNNING

RESPLENDENT

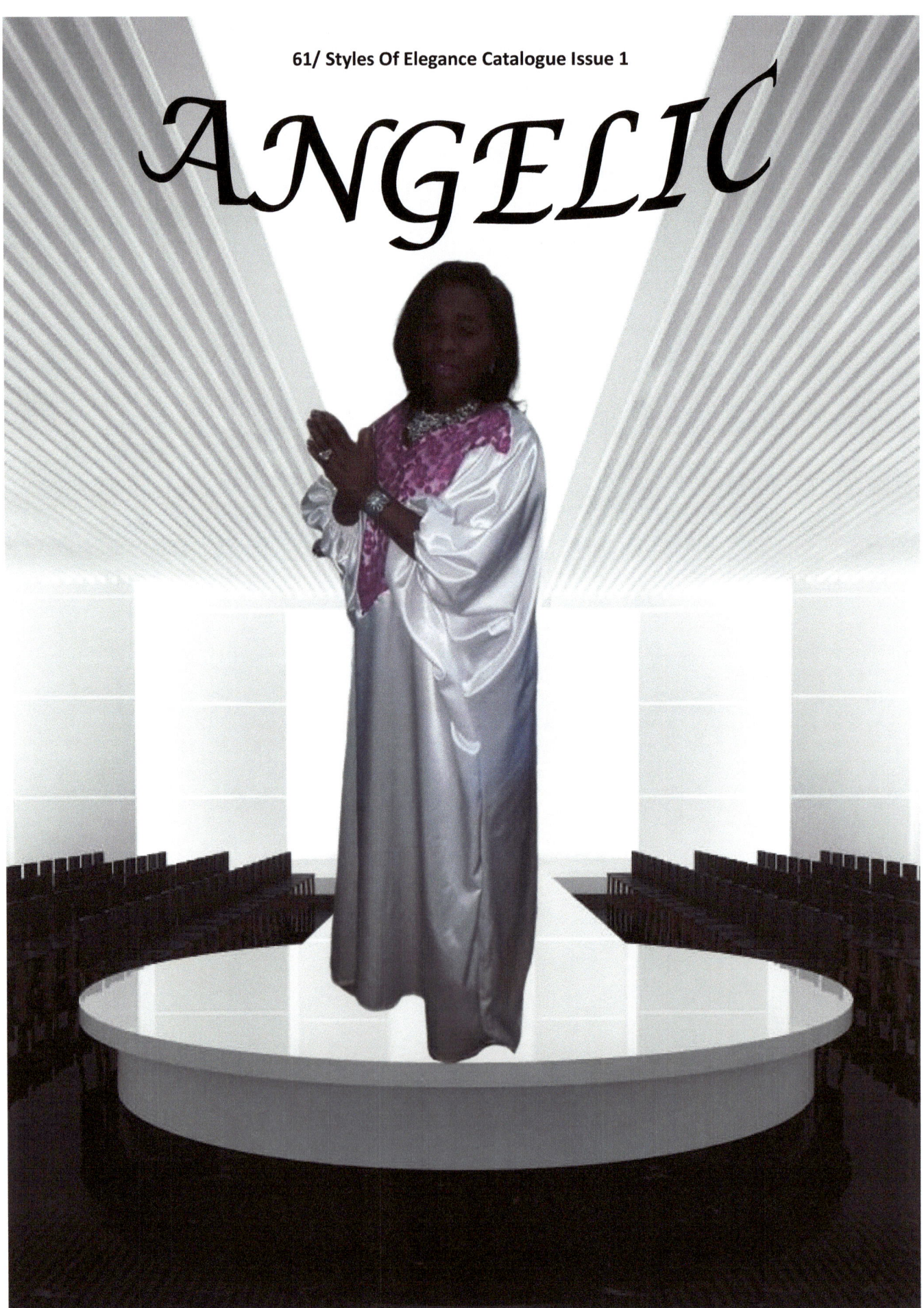

CONFIDENT

ALL OUTFITS WERE
MADE BY ONE OF
THE BEST DESIGNERS
IN BARBADOS

Mrs. Suzanne Reeves

"MADE TO FIT DESIGNS"

CONTACT NO:
(246) 850-2832